FAMOUS FIG
OF THE
AMERICAN REVOLUTION

ARTICULATED PAPER DOLLS TO CUT, COLOR, AND ASSEMBLE

CATHY DIEZ-LUCKIE

FIGURES IN MOTION

BELLINGHAM, WASHINGTON

Published by
Figures In Motion
6055 E Hemmi Lane
Bellingham, WA 98226
(360) 966-3500
E-mail: info@FiguresInMotion.com
Web: https://www.FiguresInMotion.com

© 2011 Figures In Motion
ISBN 978-0-9818566-2-9

Quantity Discounts Available
Books published by Figures In Motion are available for bulk purchase at special quantity discounts to individuals, businesses, schools, museums, associations and other institutions. For discount schedule and terms, contact us at info@FiguresInMotion.com or call us at (360) 966-3500.

Manufactured by Regent Publishing Services, Hong Kong
Printed March 2020 in ShenZhen, Guangdong, China
10 9 8 7 6 5 4

This book is dedicated to my husband, Jeff, who has helped me appreciate that each day is a gift, and to my band of patriots—Clarisse, Jesse, and Jeremy, the Daughter and Sons of Liberty.

Thank you to Dona M. McDermott, Archivist at the Valley Forge National Historical Park, for her invaluable help and advice in the costume design for this book. Thanks to Helen McKenna-Uff, Park Ranger at Independence National Historical Park, for checking the accuracy of the text. Thank you to Mary Jo Tate and Caitlin Curry for editing the text.

How to Use This Book

For Children...

Make articulated paper dolls of ten of the most important people from the American Revolution. Cut them out, put them together, and then use your imagination to make them come to life. The figures come in pairs—one waiting for your artistic touches of color and the other ready to cut and assemble.

Travel through time with your moving historical paper dolls as you act out the real stories of history or make up your own. Make puppets with string, craft sticks or pipe cleaners, or try producing a stop-motion animation clip using magnets or felt.

For Parents and Educators...

Famous Figures of the American Revolution provides hands-on activities that will inspire the imagination and creativity of your children, whether they are eager learners who continually want more or reluctant students who need some motivation to learn.

Sharpen your children's storytelling abilities and fine motor skills with ten historical figures that come ready to cut and assemble. The figures are printed on sturdy paper and, when assembled with mini brads, are able to really move! Hole punches and mini brads are available at most craft stores and school supply stores as well as on our website.

The illustrations in this book are in true-to-period costume. Two versions of each figure are included: colored pages for children who want to focus on the assembly and use of the figures and line drawings for those who like to add their own creativity with colored pencils, markers, or paint. The back of each figure is labeled by name for easy identification.

Supply your children with meaningful and easy-to-use activities that will ignite their interest in history and encourage them to discover more about the great men and women of the past. Benjamin Franklin, Betsy Ross, and Thomas Jefferson will come alive as children create their articulated puppets. Use this book independently or combine it with any history curriculum that covers the American Revolution.

A suggested reading list is included for each historical figure. Internet-linked coloring pages, puzzles, and activities are available at FiguresInMotion.com.

For Museums and Historical Reenactors...

Inform and educate children about leaders from the American Revolution as they visit your museum's collection or special exhibition. Let children take home a remembrance of their experience at your museum with *Famous Figures of the American Revolution*.

The *Famous Figures* series is also useful in generating interest for historical reenactments. Costumes are meticulously drawn and historically accurate.

CONTENTS

PATRIOTS OF THE REVOLUTION   4

READING LIST   6

BENJAMIN FRANKLIN   7

BETSY ROSS   11

DANIEL BOONE   15

GEORGE WASHINGTON   19

JOHN ADAMS   23

MOLLY PITCHER   27

PATRICK HENRY   31

PAUL REVERE   35

SOLDIER OF THE CONTINENTAL ARMY   39

THOMAS JEFFERSON   43

MAKE AN ARTICULATED PAPER DOLL   47

ABOUT THE AUTHOR   48

Benjamin Franklin (1706-1790), one of the most famous statesmen in history, was also a printer and an inventor. Starting out as an apprentice to his brother, Franklin perfected his writing style while mastering the printer's trade. He published articles, newspapers, and *Poor Richard's Almanac,* and he printed Pennsylvania's paper currency. Franklin invented the lightning rod and a stove that reduced chimney smoke, and he experimented with electricity. He also established the first public library, the first fire department, a police force, and the Academy of Philadelphia.

The American colonies chose Franklin to represent them with the Native Americans, Great Britain, and France. In England, he attempted to negotiate a new charter for Pennsylvania and worked to repeal the Stamp Act. Franklin was a member of the Second Continental Congress and helped draft the Declaration of Independence. He was also one of the signers of the Treaty of Paris.

Betsy Ross (1752-1836) was a seamstress in Philadelphia who made flags for the military. She experienced many hardships during the war, but through all her difficulties, she worked at her business and took care of her family.

Betsy's grandson first made her involvement with the flag public. He said that, in May of 1776, George Washington visited her and requested that she make a new American flag with thirteen white stars on a dark blue field and thirteen alternating red and white stripes. Betsy accepted the job to construct the flag but replaced the design's six-pointed stars with five-pointed ones, which were easier to make, and arranged them in a circle. She completed the flag in late May or early June of 1776. The Continental Congress adopted this first flag on June 14, 1777 (Flag Day). Many have referred to it as the "First Stars and Stripes" or the "Betsy Ross Flag."

Daniel Boone (1734-1820) was an explorer and frontiersman who became well known for his settlement of the Kentucky area. Boone grew up in the country near Reading, Pennsylvania, and moved with his family to North Carolina when he was fifteen. He was a hunter, trapper, and fur trader. He also established new settlement routes.

Boone fought in the Western theatre of the American Revolutionary War and served as a militia officer. He helped defend Boonesborough from Native American war parties whom the British persuaded to attack the settlements in Kentucky. He fought under General George Rogers Clark in the Battle of Piqua in 1780 and the 1782 Battle of Blue Licks, one of the last battles of the American Revolution. Boone was elected to the Virginia General Assembly and served for three terms. Through the publication of *The Adventures of Colonel Daniel Boon* in 1784, Boone would forever be known as an American legend and folk hero.

George Washington (1732-1799) was a humble but dedicated leader who greatly influenced the formation of the United States. He started his career as a surveyor and mapmaker, and then gained valuable military skills in the French and Indian War. Washington represented the colony of Virginia in the Continental Congress, which chose him to lead the colonial forces during the Revolutionary War. He transformed the army, shared many hardships with them, and led them on to victory, eventually winning the war for freedom against British rule.

Washington presided over the Constitutional Convention in Philadelphia, which consisted of a representative from each state called to create a contract that would help keep the new states united. Washington became the first president of the United States, nominating cabinet members and appointing Supreme Court justices. Under Washington's presidency, James Madison wrote the Bill of Rights, while Congress added it to the Constitution.

J ohn Adams (1735-1826) worked diligently to protect the rights of the colonists and shape the future of the United States. Educated as a lawyer, Adams became known for his belief that every person deserves a fair trial. The colonies praised him for his fight against the British right to search the property of the colonists without the owners' permission. Adams was a champion of independence, helping to draft the Declaration of Independence, which the Second Continental Congress signed.

During the war, Congress sent Adams on diplomatic missions to France and the Dutch Republic. After the war, he was the ambassador to England. Adams later became the first vice president under George Washington and the second president of the United States. He signed an Act of Congress creating the Library of Congress and was the first president to live in Washington, D.C. His oldest son, John Quincy Adams, became the sixth president.

M olly Pitcher has become a legendary name for women who heroically served our country during the Revolutionary War. Historians believe that the actions of real women inspired the many stories of "Molly Pitcher." One of these women was Mary Ludwig Hayes McCauley, the wife of William Hayes, an artilleryman. Mary earned her nickname of Molly Pitcher by supplying the soldiers with drinking water during the Battle of Monmouth. Also, during that battle, she assisted her husband at the cannon.

Another heroine of the war was Margaret Corbin, who served alongside her husband in an artillery regiment while defending Fort Washington in northern Manhattan. When he was killed, she bravely took his place and was seriously wounded during battle. She was the first woman to receive a disability pension for her service. There are many "Molly Pitchers" whose patriotic service contributed to the final victory over British rule.

P atrick Henry (1736-1799) was a fiery orator and patriot who was not afraid to speak out against British control of the colonies. He became a lawyer and was elected to the Virginia House of Burgesses. He boldly rebelled against the actions and policies of Great Britain when he proposed resolutions against the Stamp Act, taking back the right of taxation from the British Parliament and putting it in the hands of the Virginia General Assembly.

Henry represented Virginia in the First Continental Congress and served as governor of Virginia for five terms. He is best known for a 1775 speech he gave in Richmond to Virginia's Second Revolutionary Convention when they were trying to decide whether to arm the Virginia militia and fight against the British. His famous words live on today: "I know not what course others may take; but as for me, give me liberty or give me death!"

P aul Revere (1735-1818), a Boston silversmith, was a militia officer and patriot leader. He established his own shop after he worked as an apprentice for his father, who taught him the art of working gold and silver. His shop was famous for ornate tea sets, but he also made simple spoons. Revere worked as a copperplate engraver and produced various printed works. He was one of the first printers of continental currency.

Revere began to work as a messenger for the militia after the Boston Tea Party. He regularly served as a courier to spread information throughout the colonies and watched the movements of the British army for the patriots. The night before the Battles of Lexington and Concord, Revere rode with others to warn the militia about the activities of the British. Longfellow made this ride famous in his poem "Paul Revere's Ride."

The Continental Army, created by Congress after the Battles of Lexington and Concord, was partially made up of existing militias. Men from all walks of life and different ethnic groups were included in the army. The Continental Congress commissioned George Washington as Commander in Chief to bring order and discipline to the army for the defense of American liberty. Every colony supplied soldiers, who typically served in the army for one year.

The colonial militia leaders and those responsible for supplying the army lacked experience in organizing supplies for such a large number of soldiers. Despite inadequate provisions and difficulties with enlistment, Washington and the Continental Army gained the victory. Washington himself commanded approximately 10,000 to 20,000 men. Most of the army was disbanded in 1783 after the signing of the Treaty of Paris.

Thomas Jefferson (1743-1826) believed that a person should be productive and never idle. His life full of accomplishments testified to this belief. Jefferson was a member of the Virginia House of Burgesses and the Continental Congress, which chose him to lead the writing of the Declaration of Independence. He is best known for his work on this document. He served as secretary of state under George Washington and as vice president under John Adams.

Jefferson was elected the third president of the United States. He doubled the size of the United States with the addition of the Louisiana Territory purchased from the French (Louisiana Purchase). He commissioned the Lewis and Clark expedition to search out a land route to the Pacific and explore the Pacific Northwest.

Famous Figures of the American Revolution Reading List

Read–Alouds and Books for Independent Readers

Benjamin Franklin by Ingri and Edgar Parin D'Aulaire
George Washington by Ingri and Edgar Parin D'Aulaire
Washington at Valley Forge by Russell Freedman
Lafayette and the American Revolution by Russell Freedman

Childhood of Famous Americans Series
Benjamin Franklin: Young Printer by Augusta Stevenson
Betsy Ross: Designer of our Flag by Ann Weil
Daniel Boone: Young Hunter and Tracker by Augusta Stevenson
George Washington: Young Leader by Augusta Stevenson
John Adams: Young Revolutionary by Jan Adkins
Martha Washington: America's First Lady by Jean Wagoner
Molly Pitcher: Young Patriot by Augusta Stevenson
Patrick Henry: Boy Spokesman by Thomas Frank Barton
Paul Revere: Boston Patriot by Augusta Stevenson
Thomas Jefferson: Third President of the United States by Helen Albee Monsell

DK Biography
Benjamin Franklin by Stephen Krensky
George Washington by Lenny Hort
Abigail Adams by Kem Knapp Sawyer
Thomas Jefferson by Jacqueline Ching

Landmark Books
Ben Franklin of Old Philadelphia by Margaret Cousins
Betsy Ross and the Flag by Jane Mayer
Meet George Washington by Joan Heilbroner
Meet Thomas Jefferson by Marvin Barrett
The American Revolution by Bruce Blevin, Jr.
Patriots in Petticoats by Shirley Redmond

Picture Book Biography (All by David Adler)
A Picture Book of Benjamin Franklin
A Picture Book of George Washington
A Picture Book of John and Abigail Adams
A Picture Book of Thomas Jefferson
A Picture Book of Paul Revere
A Picture Book of Patrick Henry

Ready to Read Series
Benjamin Franklin and the Magic Squares by Frank Murphy
George Washington and the General's Dog by Frank Murphy
John Adams Speaks for Freedom by Deborah Hopkinson
Abigail Adams: First Lady of the American Revolution by Patricia Lakin
Betsy Ross and the Silver Thimble by Stephanie Greene
Thomas Jefferson's Feast by Frank Murphy

Benjamin Franklin

Statesman, Politician, Printer, Inventor, Scientist, Author, U.S. Postmaster General

A
Back

B
Back

Front

F

A
Front

B
Front

Back

C

Back

D

E
Back
D
Front

F

Back

© Figures In Motion
www.figuresinmotion.com

Front
G

Front
H

G
Back

H
Back

C
Front

Front
E

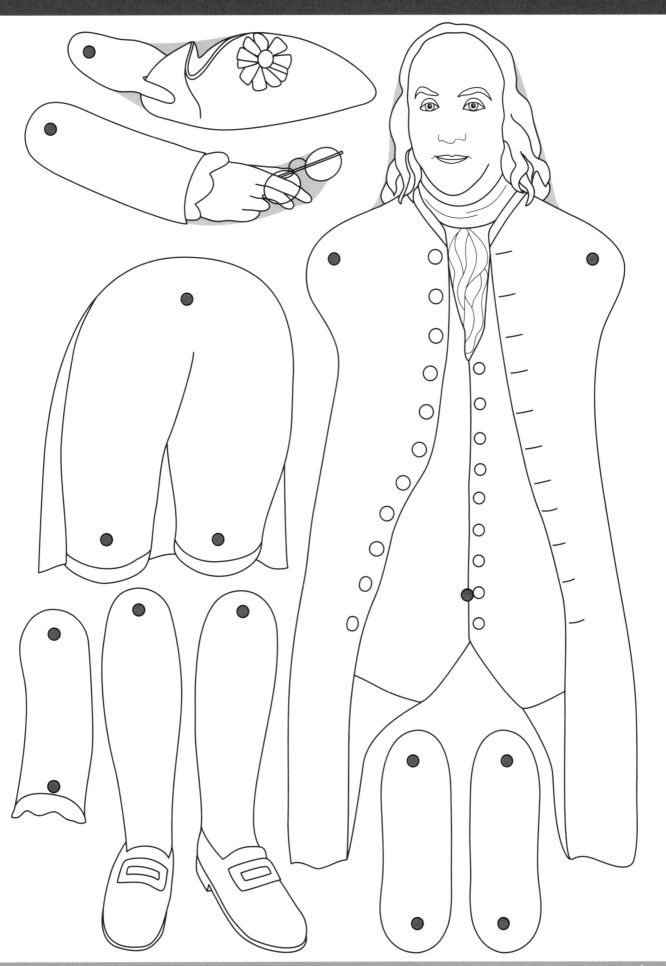

Benjamin Franklin

A
Back

B
Back

F
Back

© Figures In Motion
www.figuresinmotion.com

Statesman, Politician, Printer, Inventor, Scientist, Author, U.S. Postmaster General

Front
G

Front
H

Front
F

G
Back

H
Back

C
Front

Front
E

A
Front

B
Front

Back
C

Back
D

B
Back

E
Front

C
Back

A
Back

B
Front

Betsy
Ross

C
Front

F
Back

E
Back

**Seamstress, Flag Maker,
Widely recognized as the maker of
the first American Flag**

© Figures In Motion
www.figuresinmotion.com

D
Back

A
Front

D
Front

F
Front

B
Back

E
Front

C
Back

A
Back

B
Front

Betsy
Ross

C
Front

Seamstress, Flag Maker,
Widely recognized as the maker of
the first American Flag

F
Back

E
Back

D
Back

A
Front

F
Front

D
Front

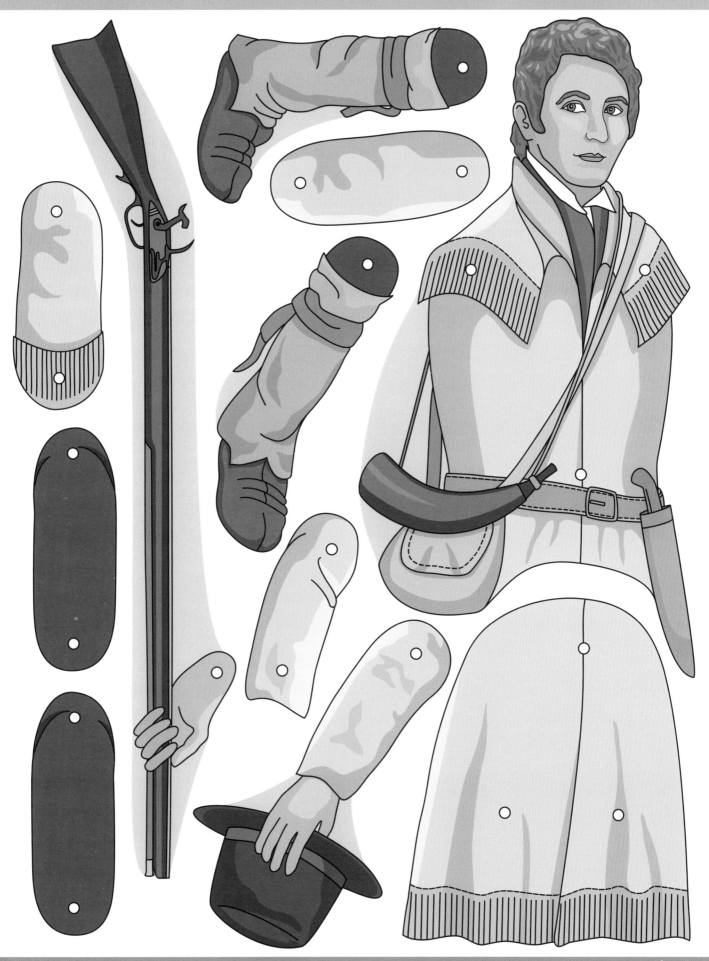

Daniel Boone

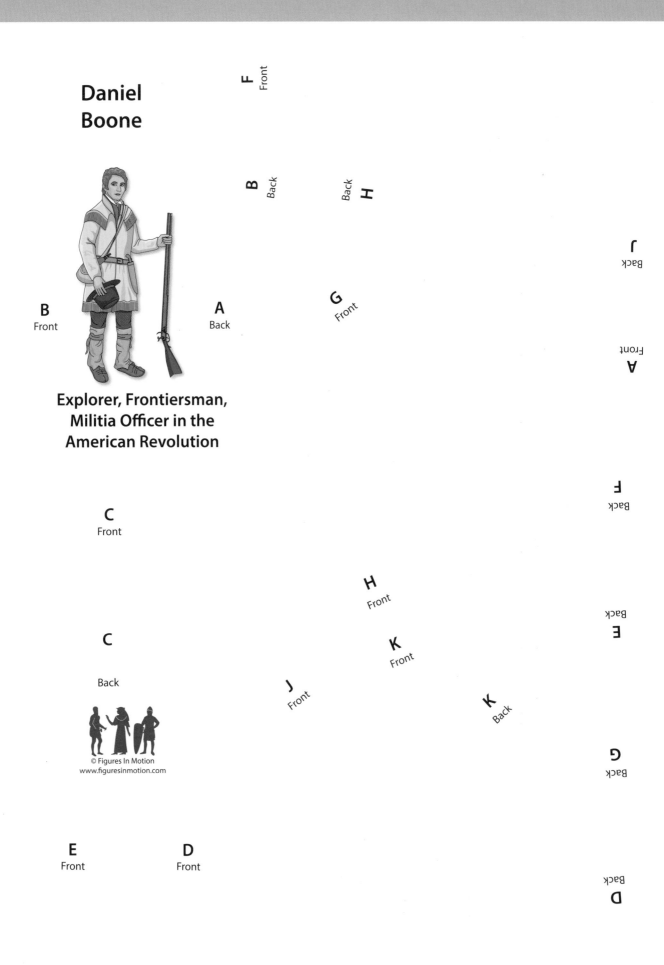

Explorer, Frontiersman, Militia Officer in the American Revolution

F
Front

B
Back

Back
H

J
Back

B
Front

A
Back

G
Front

A
Front

C
Front

F
Back

C
Back

H
Front

E
Back

K
Front

J
Front

K
Back

G
Back

E
Front

D
Front

D
Back

© Figures In Motion
www.figuresinmotion.com

Daniel Boone

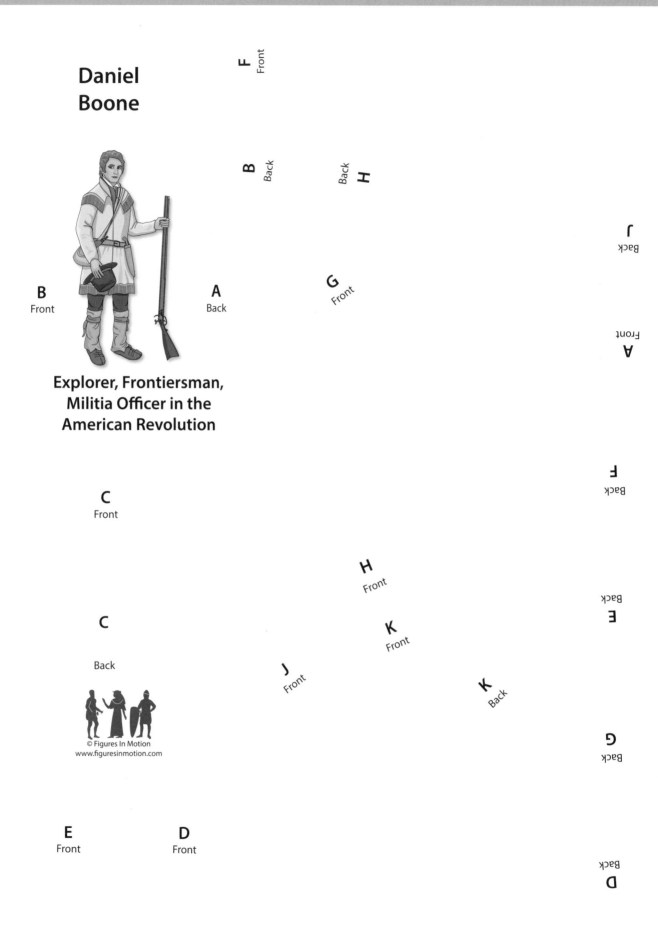

Explorer, Frontiersman, Militia Officer in the American Revolution

F
Front

B
Back

Back
H

J
Back

B
Front

A
Back

G
Front

A
Front

F
Back

C
Front

C
Back

H
Front

K
Front

E
Back

J
Front

K
Back

© Figures In Motion
www.figuresinmotion.com

G
Back

E
Front

D
Front

D
Back

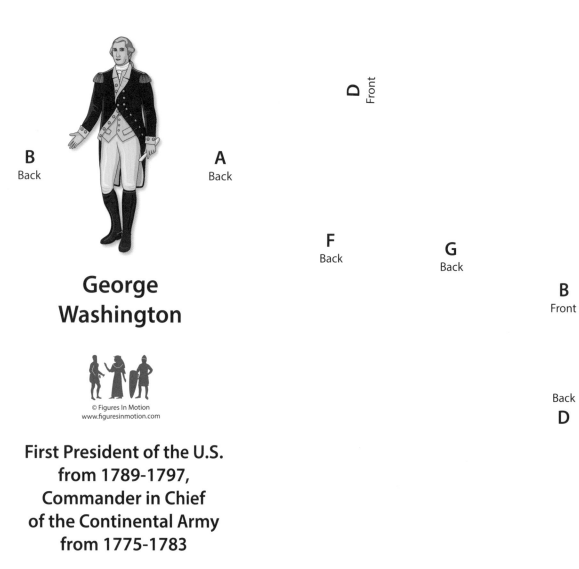

E
Front

D
Front

B
Back

A
Back

George Washington

© Figures In Motion
www.figuresinmotion.com

First President of the U.S. from 1789-1797, Commander in Chief of the Continental Army from 1775-1783

F
Back

G
Back

B
Front

Back
D

H
Back

C
Back

H
Front

C
Front

A
Front

F
Front

G
Front

Back
E

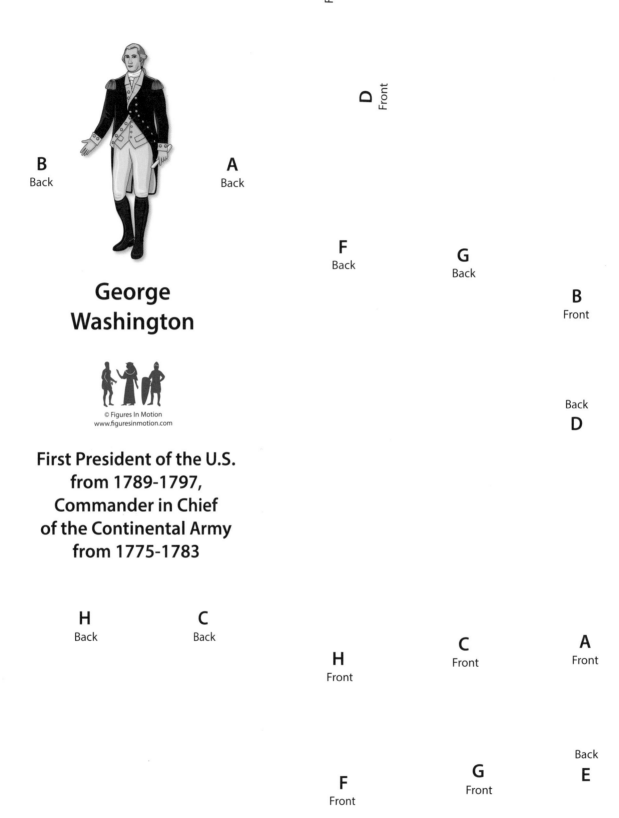

E
Front

D
Front

B
Back

A
Back

George Washington

© Figures In Motion
www.figuresinmotion.com

**First President of the U.S.
from 1789-1797,
Commander in Chief
of the Continental Army
from 1775-1783**

F
Back

G
Back

B
Front

Back
D

H
Back

C
Back

H
Front

C
Front

A
Front

F
Front

G
Front

Back
E

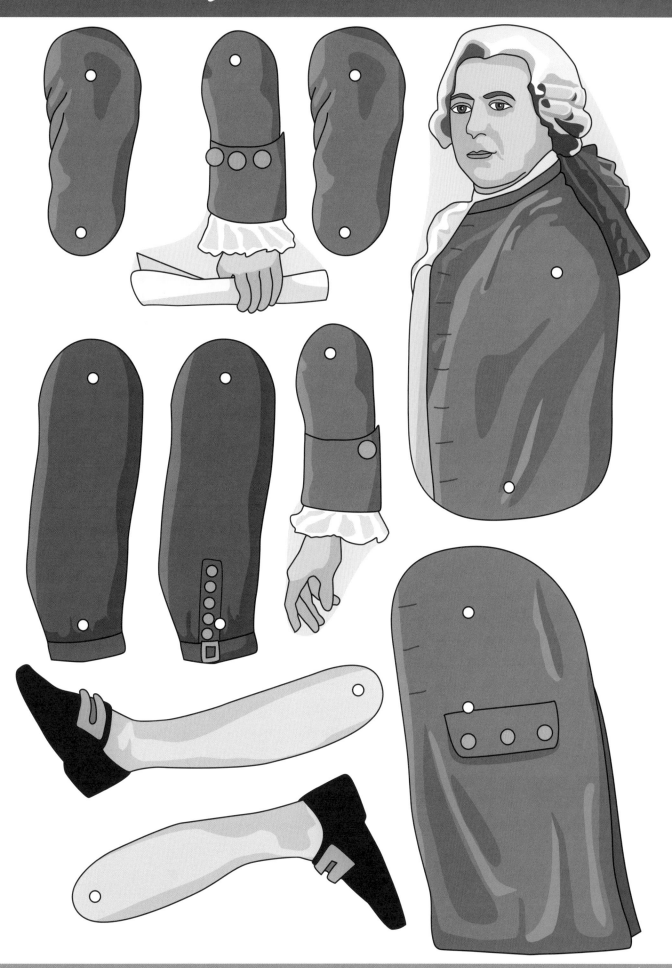

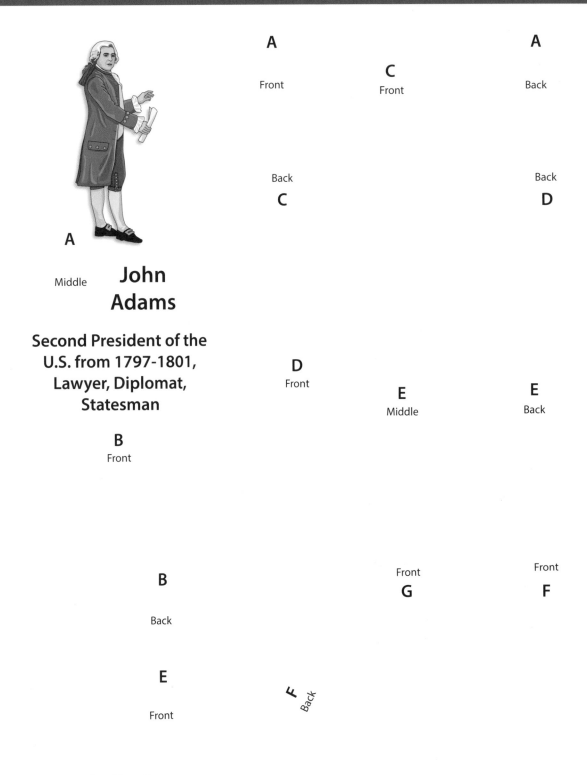

A

Front

C

Front

A

Back

A

Middle

Back

C

Back

D

John
Adams

**Second President of the
U.S. from 1797-1801,
Lawyer, Diplomat,
Statesman**

D

Front

E

Middle

E

Back

B

Front

B

Back

Front

G

Front

F

E

Front

F

Back

© Figures In Motion
www.figuresinmotion.com

Back G

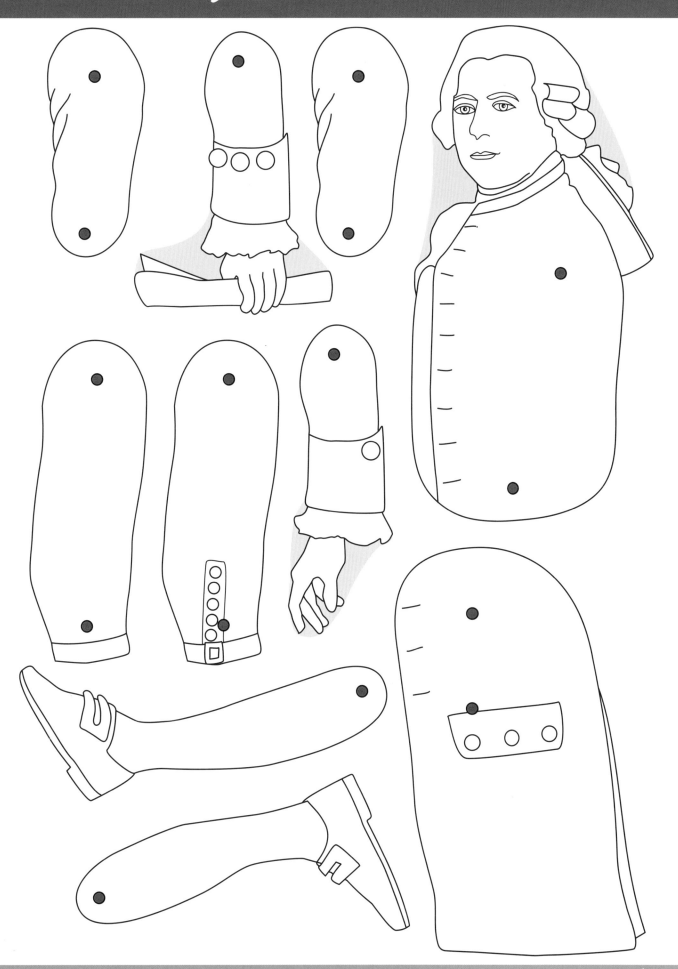

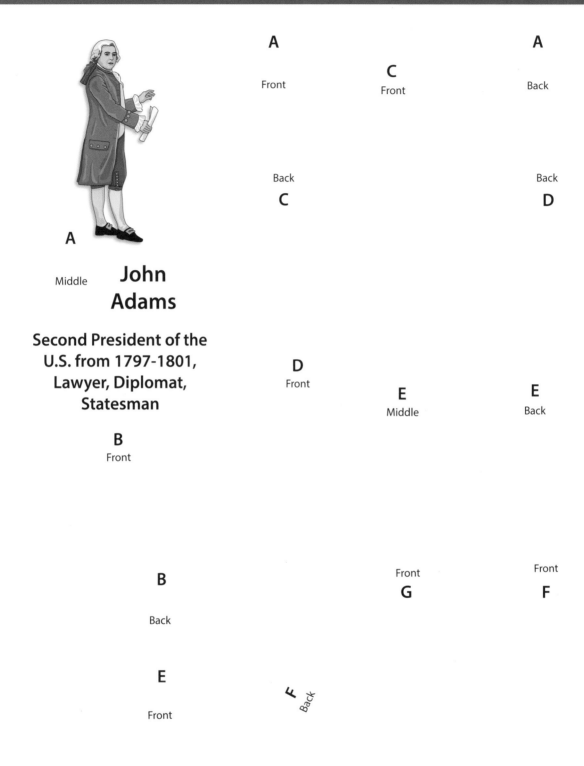

A

Middle

John Adams

Second President of the U.S. from 1797-1801, Lawyer, Diplomat, Statesman

A

Front

C

Front

A

Back

Back

C

Back

D

D

Front

E

Middle

E

Back

B

Front

B

Back

Front

G

Front

F

E

Front

F

Back

G

Back

© Figures In Motion
www.figuresinmotion.com

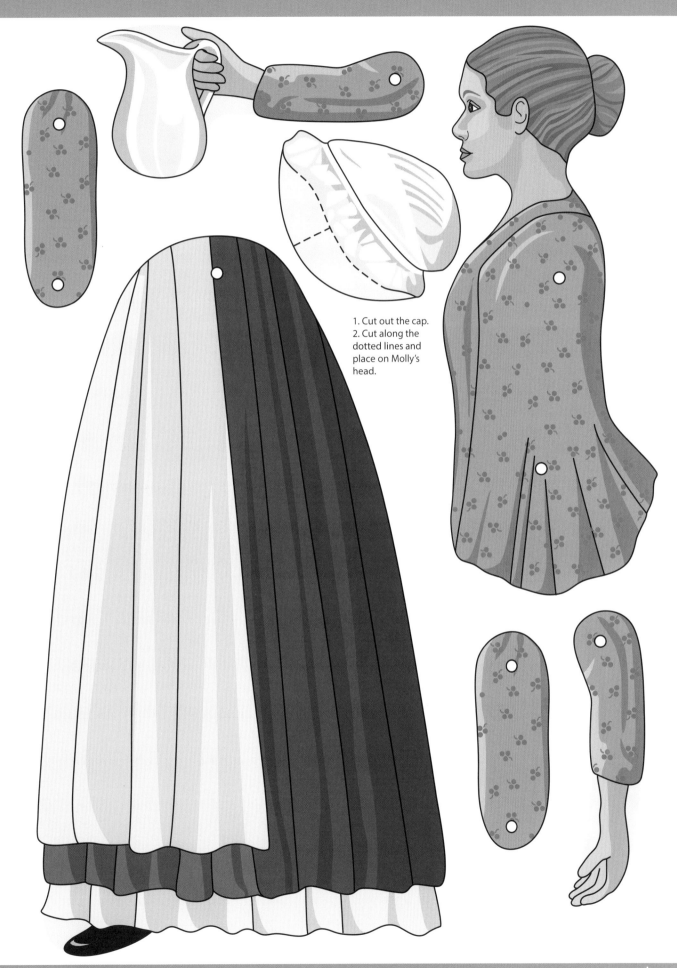

1. Cut out the cap.
2. Cut along the dotted lines and place on Molly's head.

D
Front

A
Front

Back
C

A
Middle

B
Back

Molly
Pitcher

Front
B

Legendary heroine of the
American Revolution

C
Front

A
Back

Back
D

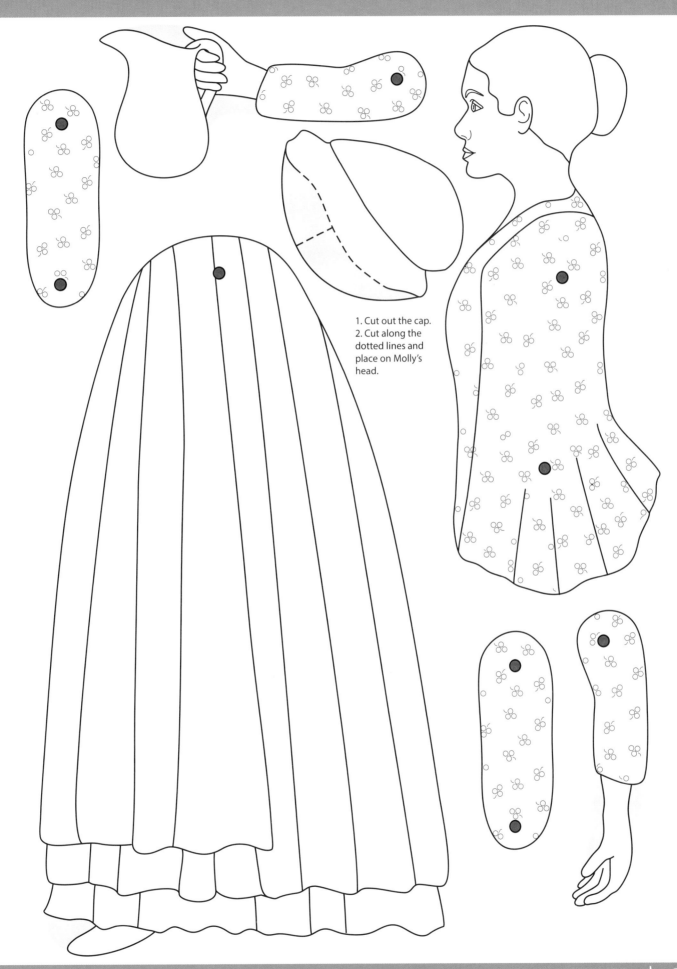

1. Cut out the cap.
2. Cut along the dotted lines and place on Molly's head.

D
Front

A
Front

Back
C

A
Middle

B
Back

Molly
Pitcher

Front
B

Legendary heroine of the
American Revolution

C
Front

A
Back

Back
D

© Figures In Motion
www.figuresinmotion.com

Patrick Henry

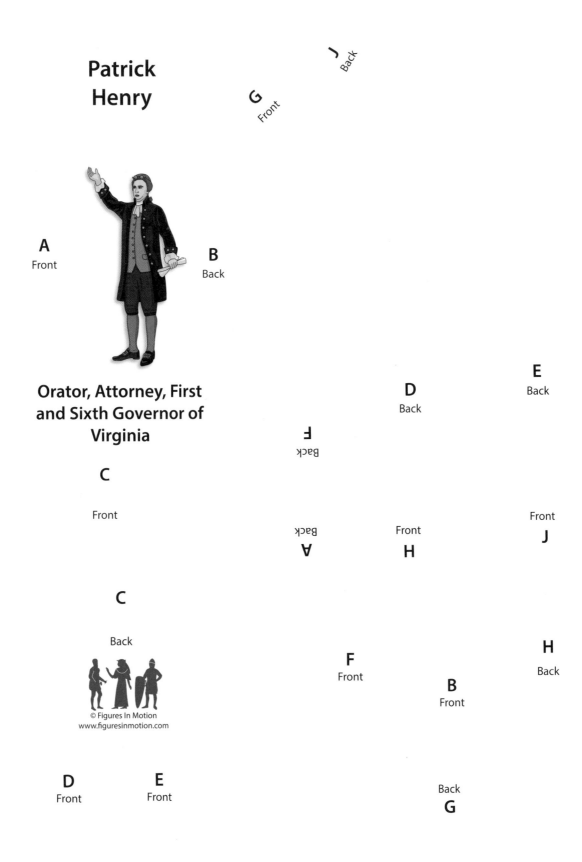

G
Front

J
Back

A
Front

B
Back

Orator, Attorney, First and Sixth Governor of Virginia

D
Back

E
Back

F
Back

C
Front

A
Back

H
Front

J
Front

C
Back

F
Front

B
Front

H
Back

D
Front

E
Front

G
Back

Patrick Henry

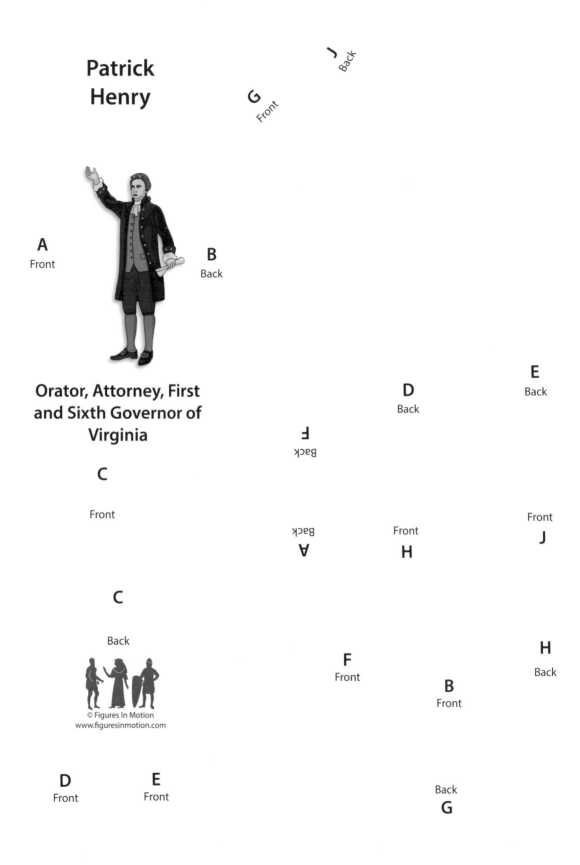

A
Front

B
Back

G
Front

J
Back

Orator, Attorney, First and Sixth Governor of Virginia

C
Front

D
Back

E
Back

F
Back

A
Back

H
Front

J
Front

C
Back

© Figures In Motion
www.figuresinmotion.com

F
Front

B
Front

H
Back

D
Front

E
Front

G
Back

PAUL REVERE

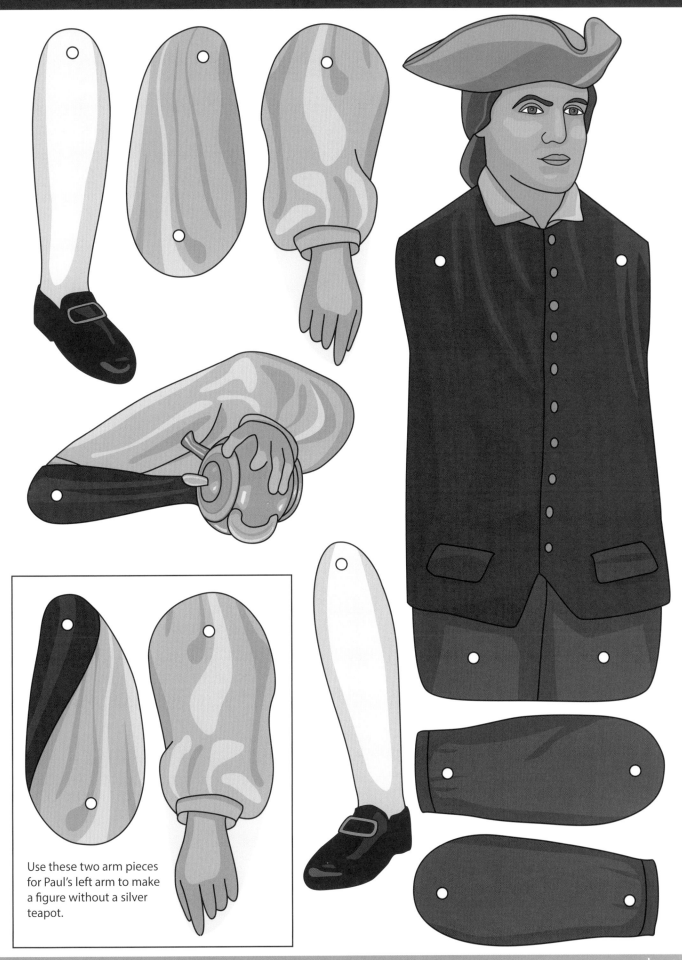

Use these two arm pieces for Paul's left arm to make a figure without a silver teapot.

Paul Revere

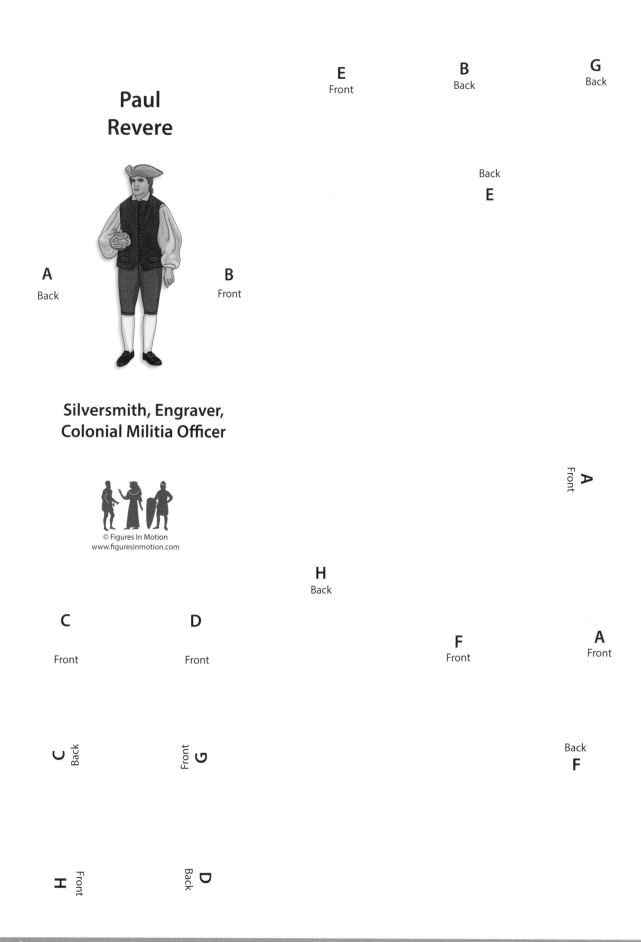

E
Front

B
Back

G
Back

Back
E

A
Back

B
Front

**Silversmith, Engraver,
Colonial Militia Officer**

© Figures In Motion
www.figuresinmotion.com

A
Front

H
Back

C
Front

D
Front

F
Front

A
Front

C Back

Front G

Back
F

H Front

D Back

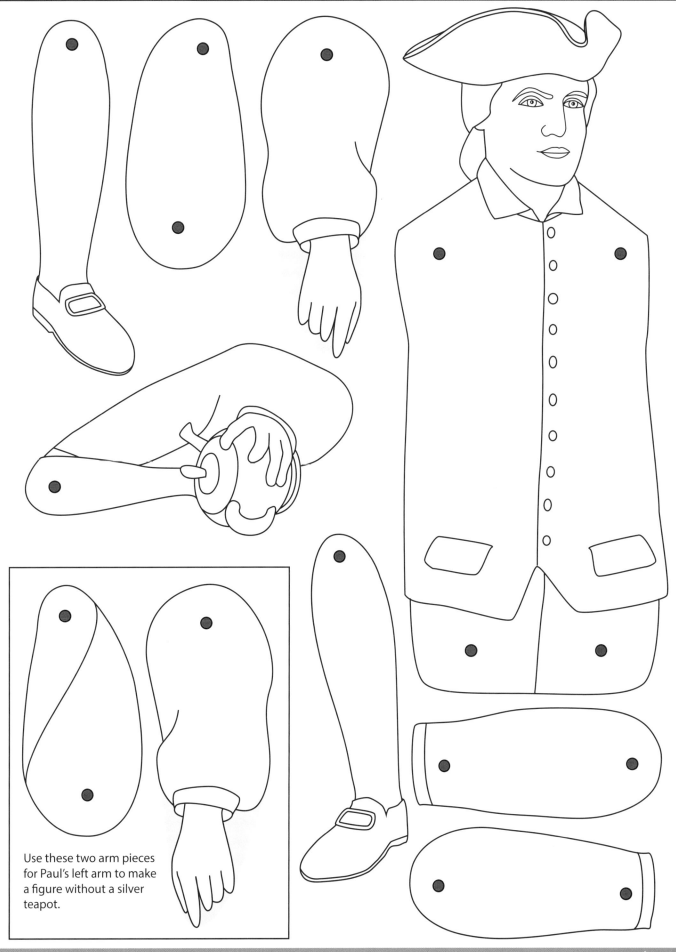

Use these two arm pieces for Paul's left arm to make a figure without a silver teapot.

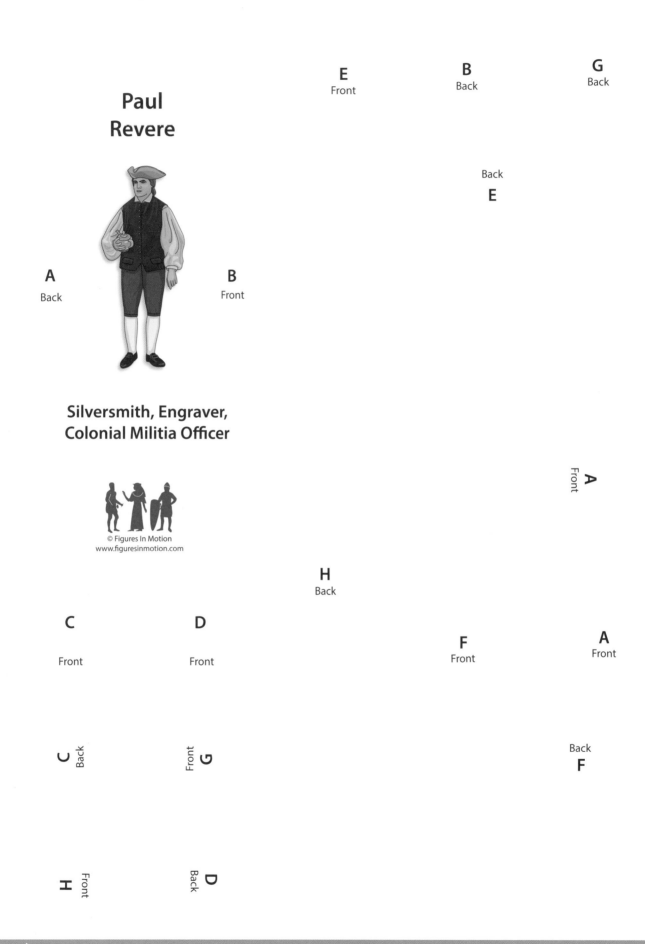

E
Front

B
Back

G
Back

Back
E

Paul
Revere

A
Back

B
Front

**Silversmith, Engraver,
Colonial Militia Officer**

© Figures In Motion
www.figuresinmotion.com

A
Front

H
Back

C
Front

D
Front

F
Front

A
Front

C
Back

G
Front

F
Back

H
Front

D
Back

The musket may be positioned and attached to the soldier's hands with tape.

F
Back

B
Front

Back
G

Continental
Army Soldier

B
Back

A
Back

G
Front

H
Front

C
Back

A
Front

© Figures In Motion
www.figuresinmotion.com

C
Front

D
Front

F
Front

H
Back

D
Back

E
Front

E
Back

The musket may be positioned and attached to the soldier's hands with tape.

F
Back

B
Front

Back
G

Continental
Army Soldier

B
Back

A
Back

Front
G

H
Front

C
Back

A
Front

© Figures In Motion
www.figuresinmotion.com

C
Front

D
Front

Back
H

F
Front

D
Back

E
Front

E
Back

A
Front

Back
G

H (rotated)
Front

Thomas
Jefferson

A
Back

B
Front

D
Front

C
Front

G (rotated)
Front

Front
F

Front
E

© Figures In Motion
www.figuresinmotion.com

B
Back

F
Back

Back
H

C

D

Back

Back

Third President of the U.S.
from 1801-1809,
Principal Author of the
Declaration of Independence

E (rotated)
Back

A
Front

Back
G

Thomas
Jefferson

H
Front

A
Back

B
Front

D
Front

C
Front

G
Front

Front
F

Front
E

B
Back

F
Back

C
Back

D
Back

Back
H

© Figures In Motion
www.figuresinmotion.com

**Third President of the U.S.
from 1801-1809,
Principal Author of the
Declaration of Independence**

Back
E

MAKE AN ARTICULATED PAPER DOLL

Making an articulated paper doll is easy. Before getting started, gather the following: coloring supplies (crayons, colored pencils, markers, or paint), scissors, ⅛″ hole punch, and mini brads (⅛″) or brass fasteners. Note: When using brass fasteners to assemble the figures, you may use a standard-size hole punch (with larger holes). Punches and mini brads are available from most craft stores and school supply stores or through the publisher at FiguresInMotion.com.

COLOR

- Use crayons, colored pencils, markers, or paint to color the figures.

CUT

- Remove the page of the figure to be assembled by tearing at the perforation along the book spine.
- Cut out each of the figure pieces. To make cutting easier, younger children can cut outside the shaded areas around intricate parts.
- Punch out the holes for the mini brads with a hole punch. The holes are colored red in the black-and-white figures to make hole identification easier.

ASSEMBLE

- Place the figure pieces face down (back side up) so that the assembly letters and figure name are visible.
- Match the letters together. A Front goes with A Back. B Front goes with B Back, etc.
- Place the pieces marked Front under the pieces marked Back as you look at the back side of the figure. Place the pieces marked Middle between the Front and Back pieces.
- Double check to make sure that all of the letters are matched together and that they are in the correct order. Some figures have more than two pieces that will be attached by one mini brad.
- Insert the mini brad from the front side of the figure into the holes of the pieces to be joined together. The prongs of the mini brad should come out of the back side of the figure pieces.
- Separate the two prongs. Press them flat on the back side of the figure.
- Repeat until all of the holes are joined with mini brads.
- The figure is assembled. Have fun playing!

ABOUT THE AUTHOR

Cathy Diez-Luckie is dedicated to providing parents and teachers with history activities that excite creative children and reluctant learners. Her articulated paper dolls of famous people make learning fun while sharpening children's storytelling abilities and fine motor skills.

"The study of history can be more than a reading or listening activity. It can be engaging and memorable. It can be designed to spark the imagination while developing curious and competent learners," explains Cathy. Her goal is to create meaningful and easy-to-use activities that will ignite children's interest in history and encourage them to discover more about the great men and women of the past.

Cathy's movable historical figures have become a popular accompaniment to any history curriculum as they bring to life time periods such as ancient and medieval times, the Renaissance, the American Revolution, the Civil War period, and the early modern era. Cathy is looking forward to the release of her new books, which will cover modern times, Native Americans, and the Plymouth Colony.

Cathy has a master's degree in chemical engineering from Stanford University. She started her career as a chemist at Raychem Corporation but chose to leave the corporate world when she and her late husband adopted three children from the Russian Federation. Cathy established Figures In Motion in 2008 and has received multiple awards for book design and educational excellence. She lives with her family in Bellingham, Washington.

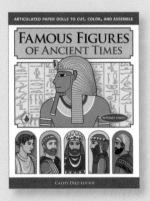
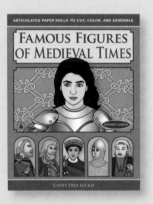
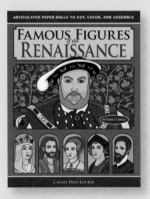
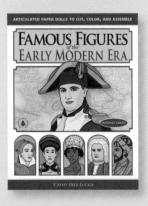
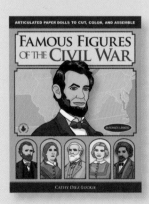
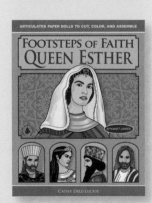